BORED
OF
LUNCH

The Healthy
Slow Cooker
Book

BORED

OF

LUNCH

The *Healthy Slow Cooker Book*

NATHAN ANTHONY

EBURY
PRESS

CONTENTS

Welcome

Thank you so much for purchasing my FIRST book. I set up Bored of Lunch on social media in 2020 to help people cook healthier and more interesting meals at home during the pandemic. And from a totally selfish point of view, it also gave me a great excuse to cook amazing meals for myself while I was working from home. In two years, the blog accumulated almost a million followers across my platforms, with video views in excess of 100 million. I am not a trained chef, I have never worked in the hospitality sector, nor do I have a background in nutrition... BUT I am hugely passionate about food. By day, I work for one of the largest companies in the UK, but I am a dedicated hobby home cook. My style of cooking is speedy and stripped back, which helps me manage my time with a busy job.

Cooking at home shouldn't be expensive. The dishes in this book are cost effective, perfect if you are cooking for a family or want to prepare meals for yourself for the week ahead. Slow cookers use less electricity than ovens and hobs, so this method of cooking should save you even more money. All the ingredients in this book are readily available from local supermarkets so you won't have to go hunting in delis or specialist supermarkets for ingredients. There should also be a supermarket own-brand version of most of the ingredients to make the recipes even more cost effective. I have included a calorie count for all of the recipes in this book simply because it's something I track.

The beauty of a slow cooker is that you can prep your food in advance, leave it cooking gently while you go about your busy day, then return to a delicious and healthy home-cooked meal. However, while the recipes in this book are designed to be made in a slow cooker, they could also be cooked in a saucepan on the hob if you haven't had time for preparation earlier in the day. Whichever way you choose to make them, in this book you can expect a lot of wonderful, one-pot dishes to free up time for you to do the things you love.

This book is dedicated to my amazing online followers – if you hadn't followed me, this book would not have been possible. I hope you enjoy the book and love the recipes as much as I do. I can't wait to see you all recreate them on social media.

Love,
Nathan

KITCHEN EQUIPMENT

SLOW COOKER

I have two slow cookers of different sizes. One is a 3.5-litre slow cooker which can accommodate nearly all the recipes in this book and is comfortably big enough for four large portions. My other slow cooker is 6.5-litres and I use that for extra-large cuts of meat or big birds. It's quite simple to pick a slow cooker as they are all pretty straightforward to use. Some of the less-expensive pots simply have a high or low setting. The slightly more expensive ones sometimes have a keep-warm setting so they won't continue to cook the food, only keep it warm. Perfect if you are hosting a crowd. Check your specific slow cooker but, generally, the ceramic pot and lid are both dishwasher safe. However, the lid tends not to be oven safe so I always take that off if I'm putting the ceramic pot in the oven.

Even though slow cookers need to be switched on for a long time, they are very energy-efficient and don't use much electricity, so they tend to be cheaper to run than a standard oven. In addition, low and slow is a great way to cook cheaper cuts of meat. All in all, I hope you'll find your slow cooker is a great way to save you a bit of money on your household bills.

FOOD PROCESSOR

Thankfully not many recipes in this book require one, but a food processor or Nutribullet can be such a helpful timesaver for making things like curry pastes. However, it's not essential because you can just chop the ingredients finely with a sharp knife. The taste will be the same but the texture will be slightly different.

NONSTICK FRYING PAN

I don't often brown meat before adding it to the slow cooker, but when I do a good nonstick frying pan works wonders. You won't need a frying pan for the majority of recipes in this book, but if you have time, browning meat does add an extra layer of flavour to a dish.

HANDHELD BLENDER

I rely on soup to get me through the colder months and often I'll have one bubbling away in my slow cooker. This saves hob space, helps with meal prep and means I can use up any sad-looking vegetables instead of throwing them out. I like blended soups rather than chunky ones, so I use a handheld blender to blitz them after cooking. These are cheap gadgets but save on washing up as you can blitz the soup in the pot it was cooked in.

KITCHEN SCALES

These are available cheaply online but are invaluable when following a recipe, particularly if you're keeping an eye on the calories in your meal. When measuring pasta and rice for the slow cooker, it's good to get the measurements exact. My scales aren't fancy at all – they are small and flat so easily stored away.

PANTRY ESSENTIALS

Here I've included a list of some of my most-used ingredients that I try to have on hand so that I can create tasty, healthy food at home. It's not an exhaustive list and you definitely don't need to go out and buy them all at once. These are just some of the staples I aim to have in stock and recommend that you do too.

I don't come from the food or fitness background but I do believe in tracking calories to suit your nutritional needs and goals. There are lots of apps online that will recommend your ideal calorie count based on your height and weight. I've included the calorie count of these recipes to help them fit into your lifestyle, whether you're trying to reduce or maintain your calorie target for the day.

FOR FLAVOUR

- Dried herbs – oregano, basil, thyme, rosemary, coriander
- Paprika, chilli flakes, garlic granules, onion granules, chilli powder
- Salt and pepper

FOR FAKEAWAY RECIPES

- Soy sauce, hoisin sauce, honey, rice vinegar, tins of reduced-fat coconut milk, sriracha, peanut butter
- Garlic and ginger – use fresh, dried, frozen or purée from a jar

SAUCE ESSENTIALS

- Stocks including veg, chicken and beef
- Cornflour to help you thicken a sauce
- Tins of chopped tomatoes or passata
- Tomato purée
- Worcestershire sauce

TO FILL YOU UP

- Rice
- Lentils
- Dried pasta – for the slow cooker, penne, farafelle and orzo all work really well. (You can also use fresh pasta but this will take about a third of the time as dried pasta.) Adding the pasta directly into your slow cooker, rather than cooking it separately on the hob, reduces the need for boiling a kettle and saves on extra washing up
- Sweet potatoes
- Baby potatoes
- Beans
- Noodles

FRESH INGREDIENTS
FOR EVEN MORE FLAVOUR

- Coriander leaves
- Basil leaves
- Rosemary sprigs
- Thyme sprigs
- Lemons, limes and oranges
- Onions

FAKEAWAYS

I adore this recipe, which was inspired by the local Thai takeaway we had growing up. The smell alone transports me back to my childhood so it holds such sentimental value. That's the beauty of food – it can trigger wonderful memories. The flavour here is sensational, like a very rich satay. It's got to be one of my all-time favourite fakeaways.

THAI BASIL BEEF

SERVES 4

500g beef steaks,
  thinly sliced
5 garlic cloves, crushed
1 tsp chilli flakes
1 tsp ancho chilli flakes
1 tbsp dried basil
  or Thai holy basil paste
1 tbsp Thai fish sauce
1 tbsp sugar
3 tbsp soy sauce

2 tbsp orange juice
1 heaped tbsp cornflour,
  mixed to a paste
  with 1 tbsp water
3 tbsp honey
1 red pepper, sliced
handful of mushrooms,
  halved
250ml chicken stock
salt and pepper, to taste

1 Place all the ingredients in the slow cooker, stir and season to taste. Cook on high for 2½–3 hours or low for 5 hours. If you would like the sauce to be thicker, stir in another teaspoon of cornflour mixed to a paste with a little water.

I serve this dish with boiled rice, or chips cooked in my airfryer. Adding 200g of rice will add 260 calories.

By a clear mile, this is the fakeaway dish my online followers have recreated the most, with millions of views on social media. Inspired by my travels in Thailand where I fell in love with a dish like this, this is a game changer when it comes to flavour – and so easy to make too.

MANGO CHICKEN CURRY

SERVES 4

3 chicken breasts, sliced
400ml tin of reduced-fat
   coconut milk
1 red chilli, sliced, with seeds
1 large mango, peeled and
   chopped
1 tbsp mango chutney
1 onion, sliced
4 garlic cloves, chopped
2.5cm fresh ginger, grated

handful of fresh coriander,
   chopped
1–2 tbsp curry powder
2 tbsp soy sauce
juice of 1 lime, plus 1 slice
1 tbsp cornflour, mixed to
   a paste with 1 tbsp water
1 yellow pepper, sliced
salt and pepper, to taste

1 Place all the ingredients, except the yellow pepper, in the slow cooker, stir and season to taste. Cook on high for 3 hours or low for 7 hours. Add the yellow pepper and cook for another 15 minutes.

Serve with steamed or boiled rice and a flatbread for dipping into that beautiful sauce. Serving with 150g rice will add 195 calories per serving.

PER SERVING 408 CALORIES

I first tried this dish in Ko Phi Phi, a beautiful chain of islands in Thailand, and I've tried to recreate it here. It's like a cross between a curry and a stew, with tender slow-cooked meat and some mild heat. This effortless, hassle-free recipe takes me less than 15 minutes to prepare before work – all I have to do when I get home is cook some rice. If you want more sauce, you could add a little water.

BEEF MASSAMAN

SERVES 4

600g potatoes, chopped into
   small chunks (skin left on)
400g diced beef or chopped
   beef steaks
400ml tin of reduced-fat
   coconut milk
2 heaped tbsp cornflour,
   mixed to a paste with
   1 tbsp water
1 slice of lime
1 beef stock pot
salt and pepper, to taste
chopped peanuts, to garnish

Massaman curry paste
1 tsp ground coriander
1 tsp ground cinnamon
1 red chilli
1 red onion, roughly chopped
handful of fresh coriander
2.5cm fresh ginger
1 tbsp oyster sauce
2 tbsp dark soy sauce
1 tbsp brown sugar
4 garlic cloves
1 tsp ground cumin
1 tsp curry powder
juice of 1 lemon
juice of 1 lime

Serve with 200g of cooked rice per person, which will add an extra 260 calories.

1 Place all the curry paste ingredients into a Nutribullet or food processor and blitz to a smooth paste. Alternatively, just chop the curry paste ingredients finely and place everything in the slow cooker – the texture will be different but the taste will be the same.

2 Place the curry paste and all the remaining ingredients in the slow cooker, stir and season to taste. Cook on low for 8 hours.

3 Garnish with the chopped peanuts to give a little texture.

I used to always serve this dish with rice, but recently I developed a way to cook noodles in the slow cooker along with the sauce, making it an ideal one-pot meal and perfect for prepping those weekday lunches ahead of time. If you'd prefer to serve it with rice, just leave out the noodles and stock. This lean recipe uses reduced-fat coconut milk and no oil. *(Recipe photo on next page.)*

BEEF NOODLES WITH PEANUT SAUCE

SERVES 4

400g beef steaks, thinly
   sliced
1 tbsp curry powder
1 tbsp soy sauce
1 onion, chopped
a few spring onions,
   chopped
3 tbsp peanut butter
juice of 1 lime, plus 1 slice
400ml tin of reduced-fat
   coconut milk
1 red chilli, sliced

2 tbsp honey
4 garlic cloves, chopped
2.5cm fresh ginger, grated
handful of baby corn
handful of green beans,
   trimmed
handful of Tenderstem
   broccoli
2 carrots, chopped
200g dried egg noodles
250ml hot chicken stock
sesame seeds, to garnish

1 Place all the ingredients, except the noodles and stock, in the slow cooker and stir. Cook on high for 2 hours or low for 5 hours. Add the noodles and stock, stir and cook for another 20 minutes, stirring after 10 minutes. Serve garnished with sesame seeds.

For a lower-calorie alternative, you could try this with rice or udon noodles instead.

Beef noodles with peanut sauce

I really LOVE a korma, but they can be quite calorific with all that cream. This one comes in at just 290 calories a serving. Reduced-fat coconut milk is perfect for creating a leaner curry, giving that creamy sensation without the calories. You don't get a strong taste of coconut as the spices really shine through.

HEALTHY CHICKEN KORMA

SERVES 4

3 chicken breasts, cut into chunks
400ml tin of reduced-fat coconut milk
100ml chicken stock
1 tbsp tomato purée
1 tbsp mango chutney
4 garlic cloves, chopped
2.5cm fresh ginger, grated
1 onion, sliced
1 tsp ground coriander
1 tsp ground cumin
1 tsp mild chilli powder
1 tsp ground turmeric
1 tsp paprika
3 cloves
1 tbsp cornflour, mixed to a paste with 1 tbsp water
salt and pepper, to taste
flaked almonds and fresh coriander, to garnish

1 Place all the ingredients in the slow cooker, stir and season to taste. Cook on high for 3 hours or low for 4–5 hours. Pick out the cloves and discard them, then garnish with flaked almonds and fresh coriander.

I always serve with a naan or chapati and about 200g of cooked rice per person which will add 260 calories.

This banging chicken curry with sweet peas and chunky onions is super-lean. This is another perfect recipe for making ahead and reheating for midweek lunches or dinners. The reduced-fat coconut milk gives the curry a lovely creamy base without the calories. If you ever go to Ireland and you order a curry from a local takeaway, more often than not it will come with peas in it and I find them such a delicious addition.

CLASSIC CHICKEN CURRY

SERVES 4

4 chicken breasts, cut into chunks
400ml tin of reduced-fat coconut milk
2 tbsp tomato purée
1 tsp ground coriander
1 tbsp ground turmeric
2 tbsp curry powder
1 tsp chilli powder

1 onion, roughly chopped
4 garlic cloves, crushed
2.5cm fresh ginger, grated, or 1 tsp ground ginger
½ tsp Chinese 5 spice
400g tin of garden peas, drained
salt and pepper, to taste

1 Place all the ingredients, except the peas, in the slow cooker, stir and season to taste. Cook on high for 4 hours. Add the peas and cook for another 5 minutes to soften and heat in the sauce.

I serve this dish with 200g of boiled basmati per person for a 586-calorie meal.

Butter chicken has to be one of the most comforting dishes there is. If you don't have tinned tomatoes and crème fraîche, use a tin of reduced-fat coconut milk instead. You could also use double cream for a treat night, but that will increase the calories.

LEAN BUTTER CHICKEN

SERVES 4

4 chicken breasts, cut into chunks
60g low-fat butter
400g tin of chopped tomatoes
3 tbsp low-fat crème fraîche
salt and pepper, to taste
fresh coriander, to garnish

Marinade
3 garlic cloves, crushed
1 tsp ground turmeric
1 tsp curry powder
1 tsp ground coriander
1 tsp mild chilli powder
1 tbsp ground cumin
2.5cm fresh ginger, grated
1 tbsp garam masala

1 Place all the marinade ingredients in a mixing bowl, add the chicken and toss to coat in the herbs and spices. If you have time, cover and place in the fridge overnight or for a few hours. If not, just continue with the recipe.

2 Place all the ingredients, except the crème fraîche, in the slow cooker, stir and season to taste. Cook on high for 3 hours or low for 5 hours. Stir in the crème fraîche and garnish with fresh coriander.

I always serve this with 200g of cooked rice per person, adding an extra 260 calories to the meal. The sauce also is perfect for dipping naan or roti.

I'm a gin lover so I adore this recipe! The alcohol mostly evaporates during cooking, but if you prefer you can skip the gin and it will still be delicious. I like to serve this with rice but it's also great with noodles. *(Recipe photo on next page.)*

GIN-INFUSED SPICED BEEF

SERVES 4

500g beef steaks, sliced
50ml gin
5 garlic cloves, chopped
2.5cm fresh ginger, grated
a few spring onions,
    chopped
½ tsp ground cinnamon
½ tsp Chinese 5 spice
1 tbsp cornflour, mixed to
    a paste with 1 tbsp water

1 tbsp brown sugar
1 tbsp sweet chilli sauce
1 tbsp hoisin sauce
125ml chicken stock
6 tbsp soy sauce
1 carrot, grated
1 red pepper, sliced

1 Place all the ingredients, except the carrot and red pepper, in the slow cooker and stir. Cook on high for 2½ hours or low for 4 hours. Add the carrot and red pepper and cook for another 15 minutes.

Serve with noodles or rice – 200g of cooked basmati rice per person adds another 260 calories.

Gin-infused spiced beef

This combination of lamb and spices is just heavenly. You would never think this dish came from a slow cooker – it's good enough to impress any guest. Relish the smell of the lamb and spices wafting round the house all day, then tuck in and experience that incredible flavour. This recipe also works really well with beef.

LAMB RENDANG

SERVES 4

500g diced lamb
400ml tin of reduced-fat
    coconut milk
handful of fresh coriander,
    chopped
1 tbsp desiccated coconut
handful of baby corn
handful of mangetout
2 bay leaves
1 beef stock pot
2 tbsp cornflour, mixed to a
    paste with 1 tbsp water
pepper, to taste

Rendang curry paste
1 tsp lemongrass paste
2 tsp crushed garlic or garlic
    paste
1 red chilli
1 tsp ground coriander
1 tsp ground cumin
1 tsp ground turmeric
1 tsp salt
3 tbsp olive oil
1 bay leaf
1 red onion or shallot,
    chopped
juice of 1 lime or 3 makrut
    lime leaves
2.5cm fresh ginger, grated

I serve this dish with potato cubes cooked in my airfryer, or with boiled rice – 200g of cooked rice per person adds 260 calories.

1 Place all the curry paste ingredients into a Nutribullet or food processor and blitz to a smooth paste. Alternatively, just chop the curry paste ingredients finely and place everything in the slow cooker – the texture will be different but the taste will be the same.

2 Place the curry paste and all the remaining ingredients in the slow cooker, stir and season to taste with pepper. Cook on high for 3½ hours.

PER SERVING
297
CALORIES

I first tried a beef dish like this in a Chinese restaurant in Swansea and couldn't believe I hadn't tried it before – it's beautiful. I love pak choi in this recipe, but you could use spinach or Tenderstem broccoli instead. Choose a high-quality soy sauce to give a really rich flavour.

BRAISED BEEF
WITH SOY & MUSHROOMS

SERVES 4

500g beef steaks, thinly
   sliced
5 garlic cloves, sliced
10 chestnut mushrooms,
   quartered
2.5cm fresh ginger, grated
1 onion, thickly sliced
1 tbsp cornflour, mixed to a

   paste with 1 tbsp water
3–4 tbsp dark soy sauce
1 tsp Chinese rice wine
1 tbsp hoisin sauce
1 tsp mirin
250ml chicken stock
4 heads of pak choi,
   chopped

1 Place all the ingredients, except the pak choi, in the slow cooker and stir. Cook on high for 2½–3 hours or low for 5–6 hours. Add the pak choi and cook for a final 7 minutes.

Serve with 150g of cooked basmati rice per person, which will add 195 calories.

This is a quick and lean version of one of my favourite local Chinese takeaway dishes, and one of the most popular recipes I have ever shared with my online followers.

HONEY CHILLI BEEF NOODLES

SERVES 3

400g beef steaks, thinly sliced
4 tbsp dark soy sauce
5 tbsp light soy sauce
2 tsp rice vinegar
5 garlic cloves, crushed
2 tbsp hoisin sauce
3 tbsp orange juice
4 tbsp honey

2 tsp chilli flakes
1 tbsp cornflour, mixed to a paste with 1 tbsp water
1 red pepper, sliced
200g dried egg noodles
350ml hot chicken stock
chopped spring onions and sesame seeds, to garnish

1 Place all the ingredients, except the red pepper, noodles and stock, in the slow cooker and stir. Cook on high for 2 hours. Add the red pepper, noodles and stock, stir and cook for another 15–20 minutes, stirring after 10 minutes. Garnish with spring onions and sesame seeds.

Technically, for a curry to qualify as a bhuna the spices should be fried, but I've kept it simple here so that everything can be made in the slow cooker. I love ordering a lamb bhuna when I get a takeaway but you could easily use chicken or beef here instead.There's no cream in the recipe, just a little oil, so it's a pretty healthy curry, but you could add less oil to reduce the calories further. This recipe makes four portions, but it could easily be bulked up with some veg or lentils to serve more.

LAMB BHUNA

SERVES 4

400g diced lamb
400g tin of chopped
   tomatoes
salt and pepper, to taste

Bhuna curry paste
1 onion, chopped
a few spring onions,
   chopped
1 red or green chilli, sliced,
   with seeds

handful of fresh coriander,
   chopped
4 garlic cloves, crushed
2.5cm fresh ginger, grated
1 tsp curry powder
1 tsp ground cinnamon
1 tsp ground turmeric
1–2 curry leaves
3 tbsp olive or rapeseed oil

1 Place all the curry paste ingredients into a Nutribullet or food processor and blitz to a smooth paste. Alternatively, just chop the curry paste ingredients finely and place everything in the slow cooker – the texture will be different but the taste will be the same.

2 Place the curry paste and all the remaining ingredients in the slow cooker, stir and season to taste. Cook on low for 7–8 hours.

Rice or naan would be great accompaniments to this dish.

This is another speedy favourite – just place all the ingredients in the slow cooker and all you have to do is cook the rice when you want to eat. I must confess that I use microwave rice bags when I'm in a hurry. Chicken and pork will also work well here. I find honey is so important in some of these spiced meat dishes, adding sweetness to the sauce and thickening it without having to use too much cornflour.

HONEY SESAME BEEF

SERVES 4

400g diced beef
5 garlic cloves, chopped
1 red onion, chopped
a few spring onions,
   chopped
1 tsp chilli powder (optional)
6 tbsp soy sauce
5 tbsp honey
1 tsp Chinese 5 spice

250ml chicken stock
1 tbsp sesame oil
1 tbsp cornflour, mixed to a
   paste with 1 tbsp water
1 red pepper, sliced
sesame seeds and extra
   chopped spring onions,
   to garnish

1 Place all the ingredients, except the red pepper, in the slow cooker and stir. Cook on high for 3 hours or low for 5 hours. Add the red pepper and cook for another 15 minutes. Garnish with sesame seeds and chopped spring onions.

I usually enjoy this dish with boiled rice or microwave rice bags. In 200g of rice there are 260 calories so this will be in addition.

PER SERVING
501
CALORIES

Bored of Sunday lunch? Shake it up a bit and try slow cooking your beef brisket using this delicious combination of spices. This succulent shredded beef is perfect with simple rice, but is versatile enough to be used in many different ways, as you can see below.

SPICED BEEF BRISKET

SERVES 6

1kg piece of beef brisket
300ml red wine
1 red chilli
300ml beef stock
1 star anise
1 tsp ground cinnamon
2.5cm fresh ginger, grated
2 tsp Chinese 5 spice
1 tsp dried basil

1 tbsp hoisin sauce
5 tbsp honey
1 tsp brown sugar
1 whole head of garlic,
    cloves chopped or crushed
6 tbsp soy sauce
1 tsp curry powder
fresh coriander and sliced
    red chilli, to garnish

1 Heat a nonstick frying pan over a high heat on the hob, then place the beef in the pan and sear on all sides until just browned all over. Place all the remaining ingredients in the slow cooker, stir, then turn the meat in the liquid to coat. Cook on high for 7 hours. Shred the meat with two forks and garnish with coriander and sliced chilli.

Serve with spicy roast potatoes for an alternative Sunday lunch, or use to top fried rice or noodles. This beef is also great for filling pitta breads or bao buns.

These gorgeous lemongrass-infused noodles are stunning, perfect for a low-calorie summer lunch. I love the clean, fresh flavour of lemongrass, which transports me back to my travels. While you are enjoying this, it's easy to close your eyes and imagine you are somewhere far away.

LEMONGRASS CHICKEN NOODLES

SERVES 4

3 chicken breasts, cut into chunks
400ml tin of reduced-fat coconut milk
zest from 2 limes
1 tbsp dark soy sauce
4 garlic cloves, crushed
1 tsp ground ginger
2 lemongrass stalks
juice of 1 lemon
2 tbsp honey
1 red chilli, sliced

2 tbsp rice vinegar
1 tbsp curry powder
handful of baby corn
handful of mangetout or sugarsnaps
200g flat rice noodles, cooked according to packet instructions
fresh coriander, lime slices and chopped peanuts, to garnish

1 Place all the ingredients, except the noodles, in the slow cooker and stir. Cook on high for 3 hours. Stir in the cooked noodles and garnish with coriander, lime slices and some chopped peanuts.

There isn't enough liquid here to cook the noodles in the slow cooker, but if you'd like to do it all in one pot, you could add another tin of coconut milk at the start.

I'm obsessed – and I mean obsessed – with this recipe. There are so many wonderful flavours in this soup and the slow cooker really elevates them. Make a batch on Sunday to enjoy through the week, or just make it on the day you fancy it. The noodles make this more filling than your usual soup.

VIETNAMESE BEEF PHO

SERVES 4

400g beef steaks, thinly sliced
a few spring onions, chopped
1 cinnamon stick
2.5cm fresh ginger, grated
zest and juice of 1 lime
1 tbsp hoisin sauce

1 star anise
4 garlic cloves, sliced
900ml beef stock
1 red chilli, seeds removed
200g rice noodles
salt and pepper, to taste
fresh coriander and lime wedges, to garnish

1 If you have time, heat a nonstick frying pan over a high heat on the hob, then place the beef and spring onions in the pan and sear for about a minute until just browned all over. If you're in a hurry, just skip this step.

2 Place all the ingredients, except the noodles, in the slow cooker, stir and season to taste. Cook on high for 1¼ hours. Add the noodles, stir and cook for another 20 minutes, stirring after 10 minutes. Remove the cinnamon stick and star anise and garnish with lime wedges and some fresh coriander.

I first discovered Sloppy Joes while wondering what to do with leftover Bolognese and here we are now. I have evolved this recipe over time and it's always a crowd pleaser – gorgeous well-marinated beef in a bun with sweet sliced onion and tangy gherkins is just everything ... sloppy, tasty, filling and low in calories.

AMERICAN SLOPPY JOES

MAKES 8

800g lean beef mince

4 garlic cloves, crushed

1 green pepper, finely chopped

1 tbsp Worcestershire sauce

700g passata or 400g tin of chopped tomatoes

5 tbsp tomato ketchup

1 tsp hot sauce

1 onion, chopped

1 tbsp brown sugar

1 tbsp Dijon mustard

1 tbsp Italian seasoning

salt and pepper, to taste

8 brioche burger buns, sliced red onion and pickled gherkins, to serve

1 If you have time, heat a nonstick frying pan over a high heat on the hob, then place the mince in the pan and sear until browned all over, breaking up the meat. Drain off any excess fat. If you're in a hurry, just skip this step.

2 Place all the ingredients in the slow cooker, stir and season to taste. Cook on high for 3 hours or low for 4–5 hours. Divide the meat between the buns and top with red onion and some pickled gherkins.

For the cheese lovers in the house, add a slice of Cheddar to the buns.

WEEKDAY DINNERS

This pasta was inspired by the flavours of chicken fajitas, which I love. The key to successful pasta in the slow cooker is to stir the pasta only once or twice so it doesn't lose its shape. If you are short on time, use a premade fajita spice mix instead of the dried spices.

TEX MEX CHICKEN PASTA

SERVES 4

3 chicken breasts, cut into
   chunks
1 tsp ground cumin
1 tsp dried oregano
1 tsp chilli powder
1 tbsp paprika
5 garlic cloves, crushed
1 onion, chopped
2 x 400g tins of chopped
   tomatoes

½ red pepper, chopped
150ml soured cream
300g dried penne pasta
200ml hot chicken stock
100g Cheddar cheese,
   grated
salt and pepper, to taste
fresh coriander, to garnish

1 Place the chicken, herbs and spices, garlic, onion and tomatoes in the slow cooker, stir and season to taste. Cook on high for 3 hours. Add the red pepper, soured cream, pasta and stock, stir and cook for another 50 minutes. Stir in the cheese and garnish with fresh coriander.

I normally serve this pasta with some guacamole and extra soured cream to give it mega fajita vibes. My recipe for guacamole is on page 87.

Pasta always goes down a treat, so here is a really simple way to make a pasta bake, with added greens too. This one-pot, low-calorie version will soon become one of your teatime favourites. Believe it or not, a tin of chicken soup works well in place of the crème fraîche.

CHICKEN & BROCCOLI PASTA BAKE

SERVES 4

3 chicken breasts, cut into chunks
1 tsp paprika
1 tbsp Italian seasoning
1 tsp grated nutmeg
handful of fresh parsley, chopped
1 tsp crushed garlic or garlic paste
1 onion, chopped
900ml hot chicken stock

large handful of chopped Tenderstem broccoli
350g dried penne pasta
2 tbsp low-fat crème fraîche
small handful of breadcrumbs
small handful of grated Parmesan cheese
70g mozzarella, grated
salt and pepper, to taste

1 Place the chicken, herbs and spices, garlic and onion in the slow cooker with one-third of the stock, stir and season to taste. Cook on high for 2 hours. Add the broccoli, pasta and remaining stock, stir and cook for another 45 minutes.

2 Stir in the crème fraîche, top the pasta with the breadcrumbs, Parmesan and mozzarella and cook for another 10 minutes to melt the cheese. If you have an ovenproof slow cooker pot, place it without the lid into a preheated oven at 180°C for 7–10 minutes to crisp the topping.

Tender, flaky salmon in a coconut sauce ... tell me something more desirable. The key to this recipe is not to stir the salmon so the fillets stay whole. I adore this dish and know you will too – it might even impress the picky eaters who don't usually go for fish.

COCONUT SALMON

SERVES 4

4 x 90g salmon fillets
   or 1 large piece
400ml tin of reduced-fat
   coconut milk
handful of fresh basil leaves
2 tbsp Thai red curry paste
1 tbsp curry powder
juice of 1 lime

handful of fresh coriander
5cm fresh ginger, grated
4 garlic cloves, crushed
1 tsp chilli powder
salt and pepper, to taste
lemon slices and extra fresh
   basil leaves, to garnish

1 If you want crispy skin on your salmon, heat a nonstick frying pan over a high heat on the hob, then place the salmon in the pan skin side down and sear briefly for 30-60 seconds until crisp. If you have skinless salmon, just skip this step.

2 Place all the ingredients in the slow cooker, stir and season to taste. If you have small fillets of salmon, cook on low for 2 hours; if you have one large piece of salmon, cook for 3–4 hours.

3 Garnish with lemon slices and basil leaves.

This salmon is perfect with salad, couscous or even rice – 100g of cooked couscous per person adds an extra 112 calories.

I love risotto and every Halloween I make sure to buy a nice edible pumpkin. You don't need to wait until Halloween to make this risotto, though, you can buy butternut squash all year round and it makes a great substitute. This sweet risotto may seem light, but it really fills you up.

PUMPKIN RISOTTO

SERVES 4

1 edible pumpkin or butternut squash, about 1kg, peeled and chopped
1 tbsp oil
1 tbsp honey
1 onion, chopped
4 garlic cloves, chopped
1 tsp dried sage
1 tsp grated nutmeg

300g risotto rice, such as arborio
1.3 litres vegetable stock
60g Parmesan cheese, grated
salt and pepper, to taste
chopped pecans and extra Parmesan cheese, to garnish

1 Place the pumpkin on a baking sheet with the oil and honey, toss to coat, season to taste and roast in a preheated oven at 180°C for 25 minutes.

2 Place the pumpkin with all the remaining ingredients, except the Parmesan, in the slow cooker, stir and season to taste. Cook on high for 2 hours, stirring from time to time, until nearly all the stock has been absorbed.

3 Add the grated Parmesan and stir well. Garnish with chopped pecans and more Parmesan.

I LOVE the combination of potatoes and garlic. Add some Cajun-spiced chicken thighs and a buttery Parmesan sauce and I'm in heaven with every bite. The thought of the chicken falling off the bone into those garlicky juices is making me salivate as I'm writing...

GARLIC PARMESAN CHICKEN
WITH POTATOES

SERVES 4

8–10 chicken thighs
1 tbsp Cajun seasoning
500g baby potatoes, cut into
    small cubes (skin left on)
70g Parmesan cheese,
    grated, plus extra to
    garnish
6 garlic cloves, crushed
150g low-fat butter

2 sprigs of fresh rosemary
1 tsp dried oregano
handful of fresh parsley, plus
    extra to garnish
1 slice of lemon
1 tbsp cornflour, mixed to
    a paste with 1 tbsp water
    (optional)
salt and pepper, to taste

This is a summery dish which goes really well with couscous and salad. It's even more delicious when you can sit outside and enjoy it in the sunshine.

1 Season the chicken thighs with salt, pepper and the Cajun seasoning. Heat a nonstick frying pan over a high heat on the hob, then place the chicken in the pan and sear for about 2 minutes, until browned all over.

2 Place the potatoes in the slow cooker and sprinkle with salt, pepper, half of the Parmesan and the garlic. Dot with the butter, add the rosemary sprigs and arrange the chicken thighs on top. Sprinkle with the remaining Parmesan, the oregano and parsley. Throw in a slice of lemon and cook on high for 4 hours. If you would like the sauce to be thicker, stir in the cornflour paste.

3 Garnish with the extra Parmesan and parsley and serve. I love this with some steamed green beans on the side.

Ratatouille is a traditional French dish and was mainly enjoyed by those who couldn't afford meat. What might have started out as 'poor man's stew' is now a staple vegetarian dish that you find on lots of restaurant menus. I love it! I always feel so good after a bowl of this as it's pure veg, and it's so filling too. This recipe makes lots of sauce so feel free to add in any extra veg you have around that needs using up.

VEGETABLE RATATOUILLE

SERVES 4

2 peppers, sliced
2 courgettes, cut into chunks
2 aubergines, cut into chunks
2 red onions, cut into thick
  chunks
1 tbsp olive oil
4 garlic cloves
400g tin of chopped
  tomatoes

700g passata
1 handful cherry tomatoes,
  halved (you can use
  sundried)
2 sprigs fresh rosemary
2 sprigs fresh thyme
2 tbsp good-quality balsamic
  vinegar
fresh basil, to garnish

1 Add everything to the slow cooker except the basil and cook on high for 3½ hours or low for 6 hours and come back to this gorgeous rich veggie heaven.

This is delicious with a side salad, pasta or even just some crusty bread for dipping.

This is so easy I'm not sure I can even call it a recipe. Consider it a life hack and shortcut for all you busy people. A baked potato is such a fantastic lunch staple and perfect if you're working from home. Just pop them in the slow cooker when you get up and by lunch you won't have to do a thing. This is how I like to serve my baked potatoes but feel free to play around with the toppings.

BAKED POTATO

SERVES 4

4 baking potatoes or russet
  potatoes
3 tbsp oil
butter
50g Cheddar cheese
  (optional)

spring onions or chives,
  chopped
sea salt flakes and pepper,
  to taste

1 Pierce each of the potatoes with a fork and add to a square of foil.

2 Drizzle with some oil and season with sea salt and pepper.

3 Use the foil to massage and fully coat the potatoes then wrap into a ball.

4 Add to your slow cooker and cook on high for 5-6 hours.

5 Remove, cut open and top with butter, cheese, if you like, and a sprinkle of spring onions or chives.

I adore anything with peanut butter in it. The lime, chilli and curry powder give this dish such a great flavour profile and the long, slow cooking makes the chicken taste even more incredible. I often cook this for my friends and it always goes down a treat. If you like a thicker sauce, add the optional cornflour paste in the ingredients.

CHICKEN AND PEANUT CURRY

SERVES 3

3 chicken breasts or 6 thighs, cut into chunks
juice of 1 lime
4 tbsp peanut butter
handful of fresh coriander
4 garlic cloves, crushed
1 tbsp curry powder
400ml tin of reduced-fat coconut milk
2 tbsp soy sauce

1 red bird's eye chilli
1 tbsp cornflour, mixed to a paste with 1 tbsp water (optional)
salt and pepper, to taste
chopped spring onions, chopped peanuts, chopped red chilli and fresh coriander, to garnish

1 Place all the ingredients in the slow cooker, stir and season to taste. Cook on high for 3–4 hours or low for 6–7 hours. Garnish with spring onions, peanuts, chilli and fresh coriander.

Serve 150g of cooked rice per person for a 660-calorie meal.

PER SERVING
365
CALORIES

It's no secret that duck and orange are perfect partners and this recipe will convert even those few people who still need persuading. It's simple to make and gorgeous. If you like a thicker sauce, add the optional cornflour paste.

SOY & ORANGE DUCK

SERVES 4

4 duck breasts
1 large orange, sliced
4 tbsp dark soy sauce
4 tbsp honey
1 tsp ground ginger
1–2 tbsp cornflour, mixed to
   a paste with 1 tbsp water
   (optional)

4 garlic cloves, crushed
200ml orange juice
1 tsp chilli powder
salt and pepper, to taste
sliced red chilli, to garnish
   (optional)

1 Use a sharp knife to score the skin of the duck breasts in a criss-cross pattern and season them well. Heat a nonstick frying pan over a high heat on the hob and place the duck in the pan skin side down. Sear the skin for about 4 minutes, until crispy.

2 Arrange the orange slices in the slow cooker, place the duck on top with all the remaining ingredients and cook on low for 2–3 hours. The breasts should be ever so slightly pink in the middle, but you can cook for longer if you prefer. Garnish with red chilli, if using.

Serve with rice, potatoes or salad – 200g of cooked rice per person makes a 625-calorie meal.

I could eat curries several nights a week in any colour or variation, I'm a curry addict. This dish is reminiscent of a Thai green curry, and it's quick, easy and low in calories. I'm always trying to recreate dishes from my time in Thailand and, while I may not always get them completely accurate, this recipe never disappoints.

COCONUT & LIME CHICKEN CURRY

SERVES 4

3 chicken breasts, cut into chunks
1 onion, chopped
5 garlic cloves, chopped
2.5cm fresh ginger, grated
400ml tin of reduced-fat coconut milk
1 tsp onion salt
1 tsp ground coriander

zest and juice of 1 lime
2 bay leaves or curry leaves
1 makrut lime leaf
1 tbsp cornflour, mixed to a paste with 1 tbsp water
1 red chilli, sliced (optional)
handful of fresh basil leaves
salt and pepper, to taste

1 Place all the ingredients, except the basil, in the slow cooker, stir and season to taste. Cook on high for 3 hours. Add the basil and cook for another 10 minutes.

This curry is best served with rice to soak up all that creamy sauce.

Mangetout and Tenderstem broccoli would work really well in this dish – just add to the slow cooker when you add the basil.

I've given the calorie count for each individual taco but to be honest these are so good, I could easily eat all eight in one go. This is the ultimate 'dump-it-all-in-in-one' recipe. Just add all the ingredients to the slow cooker, whip up the yogurt dressing and there you go.

CHICKEN TACOS

MAKES 8

500g boneless chicken thigh, diced
1 tsp paprika
1 tsp Cajun seasoning
1 tsp garlic granules
1 tsp onion granules
1 tsp oregano
1 tsp chilli powder
1 heaped tbsp ground cumin
3 tbsp sriracha
1 tbsp tomato purée
juice of 2 limes

2 tbsp honey
salt, to taste
8 hard or soft shop-bought tacos, to serve
pickled red onion, to serve
fresh coriander, to serve

Yogurt dressing
4 tbsp Greek yogurt
juice of a lemon
1 tsp garlic granules
salt and pepper, to taste

1 Add all the ingredients for the chicken to the slow cooker and cook on high for 4 hours until the meat is falling apart.

2 Make the dressing by mixing the yogurt, lemon juice and garlic granules in a small bowl and season to taste.

3 Assemble your tacos by adding the chicken along with the yogurt dressing and topping with pickled red onion and coriander.

I first discovered this dish in a London restaurant and instantly wanted to recreate it at home. If I'm in a hurry, I make it in a saucepan but I have found the slow-cooker method results in a much richer flavour. If you want to heighten the flavour even more, soften the onion and garlic in a little oil in a frying pan before adding to the slow cooker. If you just want to make the arrabbiata sauce, leave out the pasta and the stock.

PASTA ARRABBIATA

SERVES 4

2 x 400g tins of chopped tomatoes
20 sweet cherry tomatoes, sliced
handful of fresh basil leaves
100ml red wine (optional)
12 garlic cloves, sliced
1 onion, sliced
1 red chilli, chopped
1 tsp dried oregano

1 tsp dried thyme
1 bay leaf
350g dried penne pasta, or other dried pasta shape
200ml hot vegetable stock
salt and pepper, to taste
fresh basil leaves, chopped sundried tomatoes and grated Parmesan cheese, to garnish

1 Place all the ingredients, except the pasta and stock, in the slow cooker, stir and season to taste. Cook on high for 3 hours or low for 5–6 hours, then blitz the sauce with a handheld blender until smooth. Add the pasta and stock and cook for another 45–50 minutes, stirring after 30 minutes. Garnish with basil and sundried tomatoes and sprinkle with Parmesan.

Get ready because this gorgeous chicken noodle soup will blow you away. This was inspired by the flavours in a chicken laksa and it's something I make regularly. The combination of lime, coconut and red curry paste is simply incredible.

COCONUT CHICKEN NOODLE SOUP

SERVES 6

4 boneless chicken thighs, cut into chunks

2 x 400ml tins of reduced-fat coconut milk

juice of 1 lime

handful of fresh coriander

1 heaped tbsp Thai red curry paste

1 tbsp sweet chilli sauce

1 small red chilli, sliced

1 tsp peanut butter

1 tsp sriracha

a few spring onions, chopped

300g egg or rice noodles (I prefer rice noodles)

350ml hot chicken stock

salt and pepper, to taste

chilli oil, chopped peanuts, fresh coriander and lime wedges, to serve

1 Place all the ingredients, except the noodles and stock, in the slow cooker, stir and season to taste. Cook on high for 2¾ hours. Add the noodles and stock, stir and cook for another 20 minutes, stirring after 10 minutes. Garnish with chilli oil, chopped nuts and coriander with lime wedges on the side for squeezing.

WEEKDAY DINNERS

Probably one of my favourite slow-cooker meals of all time, this ragù is incomparable when it comes to flavour and will wow your family. Use a piece of brisket or a roasting joint and the long, slow cooking will make the meat so tender it falls apart. You could also use duck breast instead of beef for a rich duck ragù.

RICH BEEF RAGÙ

SERVES 6

900g piece of beef
1 tbsp dried rosemary
1 tbsp dried basil
1 tbsp dried oregano
400g tin of chopped
   tomatoes
2 tbsp tomato purée

5 garlic cloves, crushed
100ml red wine
300ml rich beef stock
1 carrot, finely chopped
1 onion, chopped
salt and pepper, to taste
fresh basil leaves, to garnish

1 Heat a nonstick frying pan over a high heat on the hob, then place the beef in the pan and sear on all sides until just browned all over. Place all the remaining ingredients in the slow cooker, stir, then turn the meat in the liquid to coat and season to taste. Cook on high for 7 hours. Shred the meat with two forks, then garnish with basil leaves.

Serve with 180g of cooked pasta per person to make a 584-calorie meal.

You can sprinkle with shaved Parmesan if you like. Any leftovers make great sandwiches for lunch.

LIGHT
MEALS

I rely on this soup to get me through the colder weather and it's incredibly low in calories. Carrot and coriander is one of my favourite combinations – it's just so simple but flavoursome. I use a lot of my soup recipes for meal prep during the winter and this recipe always makes the cut.

CARROT & CORIANDER SOUP

SERVES 6

10 carrots, chopped (skin left on)

3 potatoes, chopped (skin left on)

2 good handfuls of fresh coriander, chopped, plus extra to garnish

1 onion, chopped

1 tsp ground coriander

1.3 litres vegetable stock

salt and pepper, to taste

1 Place all the ingredients in the slow cooker, stir and season to taste. Cook on high for 4 hours, then blitz the soup with a handheld blender until smooth.

2 Pour into bowls and garnish with the extra coriander.

Packed with so much goodness, this is another healthy soup to give you a boost. The sweet potato is filling but the soup itself is low in calories. It's perfect all year round – comforting in the winter but pleasant and light during warmer weather.

SWEET POTATO & COCONUT SOUP

SERVES 6

6 sweet potatoes, chopped
1 onion, chopped
1 red pepper, chopped
750ml vegetable stock
400ml tin of reduced-fat
   coconut milk

3 garlic cloves, chopped
1 tsp lemongrass paste
1 tsp ground coriander
salt and pepper, to taste

1 Place all the ingredients in the slow cooker, stir and season to taste. Cook on high for 3 hours, then blitz the soup with a handheld blender until smooth.

This is definitely the most popular soup recipe that I have ever posted online. I'm obsessed with chorizo and its smoky flavour enhances any dish. Like all my soups, this could be made in a large saucepan on the hob – just bubble all the ingredients away for 25–30 minutes, then blitz until smooth.

CHORIZO, CARROT & CHILLI SOUP

SERVES 6

170g chorizo, sliced
7 carrots, chopped
   (skin left on)
3 potatoes, chopped
   (skin left on)
1 red chilli, sliced
3 garlic cloves, chopped

1 tbsp curry powder
small handful of fresh
   coriander
1.2 litres vegetable
   or chicken stock
salt and pepper, to taste
chilli flakes, to garnish

1 If you have time, heat a nonstick frying pan over a high heat on the hob, then place the chorizo in the pan and sear until browned on both sides. If you're in a hurry, just skip this step.

2 Reserving a few slices of chorizo for garnish, place all the ingredients in the slow cooker, stir and season to taste. Cook on high for 3 hours, then blitz the soup with a handheld blender until smooth. Garnish with the reserved chorizo and a sprinkle of chilli flakes.

LIGHT MEALS

This recipe holds a very special place in my heart as it was the first thing I ever posted for my online food blog. It was during the pandemic and I wanted to help people rely less on tinned food. Spices go so well with the gentle flavour of parsnips and this soup is hugely nutritious.

SPICED PARSNIP SOUP

SERVES 6

10–12 small parsnips, chopped (skin left on)

1 onion, chopped

5 garlic cloves, chopped

2.5cm fresh ginger, grated

1 tsp ground cumin

1 tsp garam masala

handful of fresh coriander, plus extra to garnish

2 handfuls of dried lentils (around 90g)

1.5 litres vegetable or chicken stock

salt and pepper, to taste

1 Place all the ingredients in the slow cooker, stir and season to taste. Cook on high for 3–4 hours or low for 7 hours, then blitz the soup with a handheld blender until smooth.

2 Pour into bowls and garnish with the extra coriander. Serve with some crusty bread (optional).

This is another of my go-to soups for meal prep – if I am in a panic on a Sunday about next week's lunches, I throw this one together in no time. It is simplicity at its finest and using the slow cooker leaves me more hob space for dinner. I always roast the peppers first for extra sweetness, but you can skip this step if you don't have time.

RED PEPPER & SWEET POTATO SOUP

SERVES 5

3 red peppers, roughly
   chopped
1 tbsp oil
6 sweet potatoes, chopped
1 onion, chopped
juice of 1 lime
1 red chilli, sliced

4 garlic cloves, chopped
1 tbsp paprika
1.1 litres vegetable stock
salt and pepper, to taste
cream, fresh basil leaves and
   mixed seeds, to garnish

1 Place the peppers on a baking sheet with the oil, toss to coat, season to taste and roast in a preheated oven at 180°C for 20–25 minutes.

2 Place the peppers with all the remaining ingredients in the slow cooker, stir and season to taste. Cook on high for 2½–3 hours, then blitz the soup with a handheld blender until smooth. Garnish with a tiny swirl of cream, some basil leaves and some seeds for crunch and extra flavour.

LIGHT MEALS

PER SERVING
191
CALORIES

I first came across this soup on a restaurant menu and my friend recommended it to me. I haven't looked back since – it's beautifully green, slightly sweet and packed full of nutritional goodness. It's also a light soup, perfect when you are controlling the calories.

PEAR & BROCCOLI SOUP

SERVES 6

10 pears, chopped
    (skin left on)
1 onion, chopped
1 head of broccoli, chopped
4 garlic cloves, chopped
handful of fresh coriander

1 litre vegetable stock
2 potatoes, chopped
    (skin left on)
salt and pepper, to taste
cream and mixed seeds,
    to garnish

1 Place all the ingredients in the slow cooker, stir and season to taste. Cook on high for 3–4 hours, then blitz the soup with a handheld blender until smooth. Garnish with a drizzle of cream and some crunchy seeds.

I sometimes top the bowls with croûtons made in my airfryer to add some crunch.

I've used this magnificent pulled pork to fill soft white rolls and teamed it with guacamole for an extra layer of flavour. Here I use pork loin rather than shoulder as it's a lot leaner. I usually serve this with rolls but you could have it on its own, with bread or any other carb you like.

PULLED PORK BUNS
WITH GUACAMOLE

MAKES 12

1.2kg piece of pork loin
400g tin of chopped
   tomatoes
2 tbsp honey
2 garlic cloves, finely
   chopped
1 tsp ground turmeric
1 tsp Kashmiri chilli powder
1 tsp garam masala
1 tsp curry powder
1 tsp ground cumin
1 tsp grated fresh ginger
1 onion, finely chopped
juice of ½ lemon
65ml water
handful of fresh coriander
salt and pepper, to taste
12 soft white buns, to serve

Guacamole
2 large or 3 small avocados,
   mashed
handful of cherry tomatoes,
   finely chopped
1 red onion, finely chopped
1 red chilli, chopped
6 garlic cloves, crushed
juice of 1 lemon
juice of 1 lime
handful of fresh coriander,
   chopped
1 tbsp oil (optional)

1 Place all the ingredients for the pulled pork in the slow cooker, stir and season to taste. Cook on high for 8 hours. Remove any fat from the pork then shred the meat with two forks.

2 For the guacamole, mix all the ingredients in a bowl until well combined then season to taste. Divide the pork and guacamole between the buns.

PER SERVING
341
CALORIES

Everyone loves peppered chicken and I would definitely order this in a pub on a night out – it might be an Irish thing, but I absolutely love it. This is a low-calorie slow cooker version and another of my viral online recipes.

CREAMY PEPPERCORN CHICKEN

SERVES 3

3 chicken breasts, thinly
   sliced
1 tbsp black peppercorns
1 tsp cracked black pepper
1 onion, sliced
1 tbsp Worcestershire sauce
1 tsp garlic granules
1 heaped tbsp cornflour,
   mixed to a paste with
   1 tbsp water

1 tbsp Dijon mustard
400ml chicken stock
10 mushrooms, quartered
1 tbsp low-fat butter
1 tsp dried oregano
80g low-fat soft cream
   cheese
salt, to taste
chopped fresh parsley, to
   garnish

1 Place all the ingredients, except the soft cheese, in the slow cooker, stir and season to taste. Cook on high for 3 hours or low for 5 hours. Stir in the soft cheese and garnish with parsley.

This works well with just about any carbs, including rice and pasta, but potatoes would be my first choice. Mash is perfect, but potato wedges or chips made in my airfryer are pretty good too.

This is another deliciously versatile shredded meat recipe, this time with plenty of sauce so the chicken stays moist but falls apart during the long, slow cook. I hope you enjoy it as much as I do.

HONEY GARLIC SHREDDED CHICKEN

SERVES 5

8 boneless chicken thighs
4 tbsp honey
3 tbsp sriracha
8 garlic cloves, crushed
   (I love garlic!)
5 tbsp dark soy sauce

1 tbsp hoisin sauce
1 tbsp tomato purée
1 tbsp cornflour, mixed to
   a paste with 1 tbsp water
chopped spring onions,
   to garnish

1 Place all the ingredients in the slow cooker and stir. Cook on high for 4–5 hours or low for 6–7 hours. Shred the meat with two forks leaving some chunks, then garnish with spring onions.

I adore this with Singapore fried rice but, I must confess, I have served it simply in a glossy brioche bun and it was beautiful.

LIGHT MEALS

I absolutely love dhal and this is one of my go-to dishes when I am having a vegetarian day, and it's sure to become one of your family favourites. The addition of coconut milk makes it deliciously creamy, but you could replace this with a tin of chopped tomatoes for a lower-calorie version, if you prefer.

RED LENTIL DHAL

SERVES 4

380g dried red lentils
250ml cold water
400ml tin of reduced-fat coconut milk
handful of cherry tomatoes, finely chopped
4 garlic cloves, crushed
1 onion, sliced
2.5cm fresh ginger, grated
juice of 1 lemon

1 tsp ground turmeric
1 tsp chilli flakes
1 tsp ground cumin
1 tsp curry powder
1 tsp garam masala
1 bay leaf
salt and pepper, to taste
fresh coriander and chopped spring onions, to garnish

1 Place all the ingredients in the slow cooker, stir and season to taste. Cook on low for 5–6 hours, then stir and garnish with fresh coriander and chopped spring onions.

Dhal goes really well with vegetables and rice, but it has plenty of sauce for dipping naan as well. You could even top the bowls with some grilled chicken.

This gorgeous curry with chunks of sweet potato and comforting chickpeas has added sweetness from the mango chutney. There is lots of sauce here, but you could add more veg and some vegetable stock to stretch it further.

SWEET POTATO, CHICKPEA & SPINACH CURRY

SERVES 4

400g tin of chopped tomatoes
400ml tin of reduced-fat coconut milk
1 tsp vegetable bouillon powder
1 tbsp mango chutney
1 tbsp curry powder
1 tbsp ground cumin
1 tbsp garam masala
1 tsp honey
4 garlic cloves, crushed

3 large sweet potatoes, cut into small chunks
1 onion, sliced
1 handful of spinach
1 tsp peanut butter
handful of fresh coriander, chopped
400g tin of chickpeas, drained
salt and pepper, to taste
extra fresh coriander, to garnish

1 Place all the ingredients, except the chickpeas, in the slow cooker, stir and season to taste. Cook on high for 2 hours or low for 4–5 hours, then add the chickpeas and cook for another hour. If it's more convenient, you could add the chickpeas from the start but they might lose some of their texture. Garnish with extra coriander.

This goes great with rice but the sweet potato makes this curry quite filling so you can just serve it on its own if you'd rather.

Who doesn't love the combination of lemon, garlic, butter and chicken? You can skip browning the meat but I prefer to crisp up that skin before letting the chicken cook low and slow until the meat falls apart. This sauce is supposed to be buttery and juicy, but if you like a thicker sauce, add the cornflour paste.

LEMON BUTTER CHICKEN

SERVES 4

10 chicken thighs
low-calorie oil spray
1 tsp onion granules
1 tsp garlic granules
1 tsp paprika
250ml chicken stock
2 tsp chilli flakes
zest of 1 lemon
juice of 2 lemons
1 tsp dried oregano

1 tsp dried basil
3 garlic cloves, crushed
3 tbsp low-fat butter
1 tbsp cornflour, mixed to
    a paste with 1 tbsp water
    (optional)
handful of fresh basil leaves
salt and pepper, to taste
lemon slices, to garnish

This is perfect with potatoes and salad. I sometimes also toast pittas or flatbreads to soak up that gorgeous lemony butter sauce.

1 Spray the chicken thighs with a little oil, then coat in the onion granules, garlic granules and paprika and season to taste. Heat a nonstick frying pan over a high heat on the hob, then place the chicken skin side down in the pan and sear for about 2 minutes, until the skin is crisp.

2 Place the chicken with all the remaining ingredients, except the basil leaves, in the slow cooker, stir and season to taste. Cook on high for 3 hours. Add the basil leaves and cook for another 5 minutes. Garnish with lemon slices.

PER SERVING
366
CALORIES

Lemon and pea is one of my favourite risottos and this version is so simple and, unlike the traditional method, requires virtually no effort. Lemons and peas are packed full of goodness and this light, fresh dish can be enjoyed all year round.

LEMON & PEA RISOTTO

SERVES 4

1 onion, sliced
1 tbsp butter
zest of 1 lemon
juice of 2 lemons
300g risotto rice,
    such as arborio
1.1 litres vegetable stock
handful of fresh parsley,
    chopped

4 garlic cloves, crushed
400g tin of garden peas,
    drained, or 1½ cups of
    frozen peas
salt and pepper, to taste
pine nuts, extra lemon zest,
    fresh parsley and grated
    Parmesan cheese, to
    garnish

1 Place the onion and butter in a small pan over a low heat on the hob and cook gently until softened.

2 Place the onion with all the remaining ingredients, except the peas, in the slow cooker, stir and season to taste. Cook on high for 1¾ hours, stirring from time to time, until nearly all the stock has been absorbed. If you prefer your risotto slightly wetter, add some more stock near the end of cooking.

3 Add the peas and cook for another 10 minutes. Stir well and garnish with pine nuts, lemon zest, parsley and Parmesan.

Paprika, cream and chicken are a match made in heaven – truly – and this is a simple dish that takes minimal prep time. Sometimes I replace the spinach with fresh basil leaves to give an extra pop of flavour. If you want a really thick sauce, add a tablespoon of cornflour mixed with a little water, but I prefer it without.

CREAMY PAPRIKA CHICKEN THIGHS

SERVES 4

8 boneless chicken thighs
low-calorie oil spray
1½ tbsp paprika
1 onion, sliced
1 tbsp Italian seasoning
½ tsp chilli flakes
3 garlic cloves, crushed

250ml chicken stock
100ml single cream or
   120g low-fat soft cream
   cheese
handful of spinach
salt and pepper, to taste

1 Spray the chicken thighs with a little oil, then coat in the paprika and season to taste. Heat a nonstick frying pan over a high heat on the hob, then place the chicken skin side down in the pan and sear for about 2 minutes, until the skin is crisp. Turn and sear on the other side for 2 minutes.

2 Place the chicken with all the remaining ingredients, except the cream and spinach, in the slow cooker, stir and season to taste. Cook on high for 3 hours, then stir in the cream and spinach.

Serve this versatile dish with rice, potatoes or even pasta. 200g cooked rice will add another 260 calories.

FAMILY FAVOURITES

Another of my all-time favourite slow-cooker dishes, this stroganoff is creamy and filling and my followers always go mad for it. I use low-fat crème fraîche in mine, but if you aren't worried about calories, double cream makes it an extra-special dish.

BEEF STROGANOFF

SERVES 4

500g beef steaks, sliced
1 tbsp tomato purée
1 tbsp paprika
500g cooked tagliatelle
large handful of fresh
  parsley, chopped
5 garlic cloves, crushed
1 tbsp wholegrain or Dijon
  mustard
1 tbsp cornflour, mixed to
  a paste with 1 tbsp water

1 tbsp Worcestershire sauce
400ml beef stock
1 onion, sliced
450g mushrooms, quartered
  or halved
100g low-fat crème fraîche
  or soft cream cheese
salt and pepper, to taste
extra chopped fresh parsley
  and grated Parmesan
  cheese, to garnish

1 Place all the ingredients, except the crème fraîche, in the slow cooker, stir and season to taste. Cook on high for 3 hours or low for 7 hours. Stir in the crème fraîche to make a thick, creamy sauce, then garnish with parsley and a sprinkling of Parmesan.

The calories here assume you will serve this stroganoff with pasta, however I also sometimes serve this with rice.

This is such a tasty dish – kidney beans and a little dark chocolate are added for the last hour of cooking so the beans hold their shape and the chocolate adds a richness to complement the spices (trust me on this). You'll probably never use mince in a chilli again – I know I don't.

CHILLI CON CARNE

SERVES 4

500g diced beef

1 onion, chopped

1 red chilli, sliced, with seeds

5 garlic cloves, crushed

150ml beef stock

400g tin of chopped
   tomatoes

1 tsp ground cumin

1 tsp paprika

1 tsp ground cinnamon

1 tsp chilli powder

2 curry leaves

30g dark chocolate, chopped

400g tin of kidney beans,
   drained

salt and pepper, to taste

1 Place all the ingredients, except the chocolate and beans, in the slow cooker, stir and season to taste. Cook on low for 6–7 hours. Add the chocolate and beans and cook for another hour.

Serve with rice and a dollop of soured cream. The kidney beans are filling, so you'll only need 150g of cooked rice per person. If I am not feeling rice, I serve this with hard or soft tacos.

Traditionally, Swedish meatballs are made with a mixture of pork and beef, but I only use beef in this recipe. If you prefer, you could try lean pork mince or even turkey mince to make them even leaner. This sauce is a lighter version of the traditional version made with butter and flour, but still tastes beautiful. Use crème fraîche to keep the calories down. The calorie count here is based on crème fraîche.

LEAN SWEDISH MEATBALLS

SERVES 3

1 large onion, finely chopped
3 garlic cloves, crushed
1 tsp oil
500g beef mince, ideally 5% fat
1 egg
100g breadcrumbs
1 tbsp Dijon mustard
juice of ½ lemon
3 tbsp soy sauce
250ml chicken stock
1 tsp grated nutmeg
1 tbsp cornflour, mixed to a paste with 1 tbsp water
200ml single cream or low-fat crème fraîche
salt and pepper, to taste
chopped fresh dill, to garnish

1 Place the onion, garlic and oil in a small pan over a low heat on the hob and cook gently until softened. Allow it to cool, then place two-thirds of the mixture in a mixing bowl with the mince, egg and breadcrumbs. Season to taste, mix well then shape into 12 meatballs about the size of golfballs.

2 Heat a nonstick frying pan over a high heat on the hob, then place the meatballs in the pan and sear for about 5 minutes until just browned all over.

3 Place the meatballs and all the remaining ingredients, except the cream or crème fraîche, in the slow cooker, stir and season to taste. Cook on high for 3 hours or low for 4–5 hours. Try not to stir too much or the meatballs will fall apart. Add the cream or crème fraîche and cook for another 10 minutes. Garnish with chopped dill.

Serve with potatoes or rice for a perfect family dinner.

Spaghetti Bolognese is one of those dishes everyone loves, and everyone seems to have their own version. I find it tastes so much better when the ingredients are marinated together overnight, or it's cooked on low for a very long time like it is here. This is SO much better than a jar of pasta sauce, and has no added oil or sugar.

SPAGHETTI BOLOGNESE

SERVES 4

500g beef mince, ideally
  5% fat
2 x 400g tins of chopped
  tomatoes
8 mushrooms, halved
2–3 tbsp tomato purée
1 tbsp Worcestershire sauce
1 tsp dried basil
1 tsp dried rosemary
1 tsp dried thyme
1 tsp dried oregano
5 garlic cloves, crushed

1 onion, chopped
2 bay leaves
100ml red wine
1 beef stock pot
salt and pepper, to taste
a few fresh basil leaves,
  to garnish
grated Parmesan cheese, to
  garnish (optional)
600g cooked spaghetti,
  to serve

1 If you have time, heat a nonstick frying pan over a high heat on the hob, then place the mince in the pan and sear for a couple of minutes until browned all over. Drain off any excess fat. If you're in a hurry, just skip this step.

2 Place the browned or raw mince in the slow cooker and break it up with a spoon. Add all the remaining ingredients, stir and season to taste. Cook on high for 3–4 hours or low for 6–7 hours, giving it a good stir half way through if you are at home.

3 Stir the cooked spaghetti into the sauce or serve the sauce on top of the spaghetti. Garnish with basil leaves and grated Parmesan.

This dream combo of ingredients is universally loved, and this convenient, one-pot version makes meal times even easier. This recipe makes three big portions, which could easily stretch to feed a family of four.

CHICKEN, MOZZARELLA & PESTO PASTA

SERVES 4

3 chicken breasts, sliced
4 tbsp reduced-fat basil pesto
3 garlic cloves, crushed
juice of 1 lemon
500ml hot chicken stock

350g dry penne pasta
1 tbsp low-fat soft cream cheese
70g mozzarella, chopped
salt and pepper, to taste

1 Place the chicken, pesto, garlic and lemon juice in the slow cooker, stir and season to taste. Cook on high for 2 hours. Add the stock and pasta and cook for another 40 minutes, stirring after 30 minutes. Stir in the soft cheese, top with the mozzarella and cook for another 20 minutes until the cheese has melted.

2 If you have an ovenproof slow cooker, you can put the pasta under the grill for 5 minutes at the end, until the cheese is browned and bubbling.

PER SERVING
339
CALORIES

Honey and mustard are one of my favourite flavour combinations. This is another of my go-to dishes – it's low in calories with no oil or butter required. If you like a thicker sauce, add the cornflour paste.

HONEY MUSTARD CHICKEN

SERVES 4

4 chicken breasts
4 tbsp honey
2 tbsp wholegrain mustard
1 tbsp Italian seasoning
4 garlic cloves, crushed
handful of fresh basil leaves
175ml chicken stock
1 tbsp cornflour, mixed to

a paste with 1 tbsp water
  (optional)
90g low-fat soft cream
  cheese
fresh basil, to garnish
  (optional)
salt and pepper, to taste

1 Place all the ingredients, except the soft cheese, in the slow cooker, stir and season to taste. Cook on high for 3 hours, then stir in the soft cheese. Garnish with fresh basil leaves, if using.

This chicken goes well with pasta, potatoes or even salad and rice. I often serve it with broccoli and mashed potato – 150g of mash adds about 132 calories.

The taste of chicken with olives and tomatoes transports me to the sunny Mediterranean. This dish is both simple and elegant and the whole family will fall in love with it. If it's convenient, add the peppers just for the last hour of cooking so they keep their shape, but skip this step if you like.

CHICKEN CACCIATORE

SERVES 4

8 boneless chicken thighs
1 tsp paprika
1 tbsp oil
700g passata
120g black olives, chopped
1 tbsp Italian seasoning
handful of fresh parsley,
  chopped
zest of 1 lemon, plus 1 slice

1 onion, sliced
4 garlic cloves, crushed
5 sprigs of fresh thyme
1 tbsp tomato purée
1 tsp chilli flakes
50ml red wine
75g sweet roasted red
  peppers from a jar
salt and pepper, to taste

1 Season the chicken thighs with salt, pepper and the paprika. Heat the oil in a nonstick frying pan over a high heat on the hob, then place the chicken in the pan and sear for about 3 minutes, until browned all over.

2 Place the chicken with all the other ingredients, except the peppers, in the slow cooker, stir and season to taste. Cook on high for 2 hours or low for 5 hours. Add the peppers and cook for another hour.

I love this chicken with green veg and couscous.

Tuscan chicken is incredible. I always cooked this recipe in a frying pan but for my first book I thought I would recreate it as a slow-cooker dish. I haven't made it in a saucepan since. *(Recipe photo on next page.)*

TUSCAN CHICKEN

SERVES 4

4 chicken breasts
1 tbsp oil
1 tsp papika
1 tsp dried basil
1 tsp dried oregano
1 tsp dried thyme
250ml chicken stock
handful of sundried
   tomatoes

50ml white wine
1 tbsp Dijon mustard
4 garlic cloves, crushed
1 onion, chopped
2 tbsp low-fat soft cream
   cheese or crème fraîche
handful of fresh basil leaves
salt and pepper, to taste

1 Drizzle the chicken breasts with the oil, then coat in the paprika, basil, oregano and thyme and season to taste. Heat a nonstick frying pan over a high heat on the hob, then place the chicken in the pan and sear for 2 minutes on each side.

2 Place the chicken with all the remaining ingredients, except the soft cheese and basil leaves, in the slow cooker, stir and season to taste. Cook on high for 2–3 hours, then stir in the soft cheese and sprinkle over the fresh basil.

Serve with 150g of cooked pasta per person, which adds an additional 197 calories.

I aim for one vegetarian day every week and when I'm craving pasta or something warming, this doesn't disappoint. I love lasagne and this veggie version is packed full of flavour after a long, slow cook. I never say no to lasagne.

VEGETARIAN LASAGNE

SERVES 6

120g pine nuts or other nuts
3 x 400g tins of chopped tomatoes
1 tbsp red pesto
5 garlic cloves, crushed
2 tsp vegetable bouillon powder
1 tbsp dried oregano
1 tbsp dried thyme
1 tbsp tomato purée
1 courgette, finely chopped
1 red pepper, finely chopped
1 onion, finely chopped

100g mushrooms, finely chopped
handful of fresh basil, chopped
1 aubergine, sliced
8 sheets of dried lasagne
1–2 tbsp basil pesto
100g ricotta cheese (or extra mozzarella)
100g mozzarella, shredded
1 large tomato, sliced
salt and pepper, to taste

1 Place the pine nuts, tinned tomatoes, red pesto, garlic, vegetable bouillon, herbs and tomato purée in a Nutribullet or food processor and blitz for 15–20 seconds until the pine nuts are in small pieces but still have some texture. Place the mixture in a mixing bowl, season to taste and add the courgette, red pepper, onion, mushrooms and fresh basil.

2 Place one-third of the vegetable mixture in the slow cooker and top with one-third of the aubergine slices and one-third of the lasagne, breaking up the sheets to fit the pot.

continues

VEGETARIAN LASAGNE (continued)

Dot with one-third of the basil pesto, one-third of the ricotta and one-quarter of the mozzarella. Repeat the layers until the ingredients are used up, finishing with the remaining mozzarella and the sliced tomato on top of the final layer of lasagne sheets.

3 Cook on high for 4 hours. If you have an ovenproof slow cooker pot, place it without the lid under a preheated grill for 10 minutes to create a golden crust on top.

This is a perfect midweek meal with garlic bread, salad and light coleslaw.

The eagle-eyed among you might recognise the flavours here from one of the most popular chicken chain restaurants, which I personally am a huge fan of. With succulent meat falling off the bone and extra-crispy skin, this chicken is amazing, and perfect for meal prep too. *(Recipe photo on next page.)*

PERI PERI-STYLE CHICKEN
WITH CORN

SERVES 5

1 tbsp dried oregano
juice of 1 lemon
juice of 2 limes, plus 1 slice
1 tbsp paprika
1 tsp mild chilli powder
2 tbsp olive oil

3 garlic cloves, crushed
1 whole chicken
5 corn on the cob
1 bay leaf
salt and pepper, to taste

1 Place the oregano, lemon and lime juice, paprika, chilli powder, oil and garlic in a large mixing bowl, season to taste and stir to combine. Add the chicken and corn and turn to coat in the marinade.

2 Pop the bay leaf and lime slice inside the chicken and arrange the chicken and corn in the slow cooker. Cook on high for 4–5 hours or low for 8 hours then place the slow cooker pot without the lid in a preheated oven at 200°C for 10 minutes until the skin is crisp. If your slow cooker pot is not ovenproof, transfer the chicken and corn to an ovenproof dish.

The chicken goes in the oven at the end to crisp up the skin, but it could be cooked in the oven from the start if you prefer – just coat the meat in the marinade and roast as normal.

Peri peri-style chicken with corn

A gorgeous, hearty but calorie-conscious pie with a dash of cream to give you the indulgent feels. You could shave off nearly a quarter of the calories by leaving out the chorizo, but that spicy, smoky flavour makes all the difference. You can also replace the cream with crème fraîche or soft cream cheese for a slightly lighter dish.

CREAMY CHICKEN, CHORIZO & LEEK PIE

SERVES 4

1 tsp oil
130g chorizo, sliced
1 leek, sliced
3 chicken breasts, cut into
   chunks
2 garlic cloves, crushed
350ml chicken stock
1 tsp grated nutmeg
1 tbsp Dijon mustard

1 bay leaf
1 heaped tbsp cornflour,
   mixed to a paste with
   1 tbsp water
100ml single cream
5 sheets of filo pastry
1 egg, beaten
1 tbsp sesame seeds
salt and pepper, to taste

1 Heat the oil in a frying pan over a high heat on the hob, then place the chorizo and leek in the pan and cook until the chorizo is just browned. Place in the slow cooker with the chicken, garlic, stock, nutmeg, mustard, bay leaf and cornflour paste and season to taste. Cook on high for 3 hours.

2 Stir in the cream then crumple the sheets of filo pastry on top – try to spread them out as much as possible so they cook evenly. Brush the pastry with the beaten egg, sprinkle with the sesame seeds then place the slow cooker pot without the lid in a preheated oven at 180°C for 25 minutes until golden. If your slow cooker pot is not ovenproof, transfer the chicken and sauce to an ovenproof dish before topping with the pastry.

I serve this pie with veg, mash or simple boiled potatoes – it's so versatile.

COMFORT
FOOD

My all-time favourite soup, and one I tried for the first time in a French restaurant in Disneyland Florida of all places. With the first spoonful, I knew I had to make it at home and I have evolved it into a convenient slow-cooker recipe. This might not be the most authentic recipe and I apologise now to the French nation – I must confess to using Italian herb seasoning and Worcestershire sauce in my French onion soup.

FRENCH ONION SOUP

SERVES 6

10 onions, sliced
100g low-fat butter
1 tbsp Italian herb seasoning
2 garlic cloves, crushed
1 bay leaf
2 tbsp brown sugar
200ml white wine

900ml vegetable or
    beef stock
1 tsp Worcestershire sauce
slices of baguette
120g gruyère cheese,
    grated
salt and pepper, to taste

1 Place the onions, butter, Italian seasoning, garlic, bay leaf, sugar and wine in the slow cooker, stir and season to taste. Cook on high for 10 hours. Add the stock and Worcestershire sauce and stir well.

2 Arrange the slices of bread on top of the soup and sprinkle with the grated cheese. Cook under a preheated grill for 8–10 minutes until golden brown. If your slow cooker pot is not ovenproof, transfer the soup to an ovenproof dish before topping with the bread and cheese.

My most popular recipe ever, this has been viewed over 20 million times and gone viral every time I have shared it. I hope you love it as much as I do. It is higher in calories than most of my recipes but the taste is worth it. However, you could reduce the calories by using soft cream cheese instead of cream.

CREAMY CHICKEN, CHORIZO & SUNDRIED TOMATO PASTA

SERVES 4

100g chorizo, sliced
3 chicken breasts, cut into
   chunks
2 tbsp sundried tomato pesto
handful of sundried
   tomatoes, chopped
5 garlic cloves, sliced
1 tsp dried basil

650ml hot chicken stock
350g dried penne pasta
250ml double cream
200g spinach
salt and pepper, to taste
grated Parmesan cheese,
   to garnish

1 If you have time, heat a nonstick frying pan over a high heat on the hob, then place the chorizo in the pan and sear until just browned all over. If you're in a hurry, just skip this step.

2 Place the chorizo, chicken, pesto, sundried tomatoes, garlic, basil and 150ml of the chicken stock in the slow cooker, stir and season to taste. Cook on high for 2½ hours. Add the pasta and remaining stock and cook for another 45 minutes, stirring after 30 minutes.

3 Stir in the cream and spinach – the spinach will wilt really quickly into the sauce. Sprinkle the pasta with grated Parmesan.

When I think of mac & cheese, it reminds me of being in New York. This is a simple, fuss-free way to make it at home in one pot, saving time but never compromising on flavour. This is proper comfort food to fill you up on a cold winter night. I use low-fat butter as you might as well save on calories where you can! Mac & cheese puts a smile on everyone's face.

GARLIC MAC & CHEESE

SERVES 4

400g dried macaroni pasta
725ml semi-skimmed milk
5 garlic cloves, crushed
130g Cheddar cheese, grated
½ tsp paprika
¼ tsp grated nutmeg

100g low-fat butter
50g Parmesan cheese, grated
handful of breadcrumbs (optional)
salt and pepper, to taste
chopped chives, to garnish

1 Place all the ingredients, except the Parmesan and breadcrumbs, in the slow cooker, stir and season to taste. Cook on low for 1 hour 20 minutes. Stir well, add the Parmesan and a little extra milk if it needs loosening up, then cook for another 20–25 minutes.

2 If you like a crispy topping and you have an ovenproof slow cooker pot, sprinkle the breadcrumbs over the top of the pasta and cook under a preheated grill until golden. Garnish with chopped chives.

This is another one of my fan favourites and a proper crowd pleaser with a slightly sweet twist to it. This simple recipe is ideal for weekend meal prep – imagine having it in the fridge to look forward to later in the week.

CHICKEN, PEANUT BUTTER & SWEET POTATO CURRY

SERVES 4

700g sweet potatoes, chopped

600g boneless chicken thighs, cut into chunks

400g tin of chopped tomatoes

400ml tin of reduced-fat coconut milk

1 tbsp tomato purée

1 tbsp curry powder

1 tsp ground cumin

1 tsp chilli powder

1 tsp ground coriander

1 tsp ground turmeric

½ tsp Chinese 5 spice

1 onion, chopped

4 garlic cloves, crushed

2.5cm fresh ginger, grated

2 tbsp peanut butter

salt and pepper, to taste

chopped nuts of your choice and fresh coriander, to garnish

1 Place all the ingredients in the slow cooker, stir and season to taste. Cook on high for 4 hours or low for 8 hours. Garnish with chopped nuts and coriander.

I serve this with only 100g of cooked rice per person to make a 630-calorie meal as the sweet potato is so filling.

Being from the island of Ireland, I had to include an Irish stew. Everyone has their own recipe, but this is how I make mine. It's controversial, but I like it this way and it was inspired by my Mum who always has, and always will, make her stew in a slow cooker because it adds so much flavour. Don't worry if you don't like Guinness, you won't taste it – the alcohol evaporates, leaving an amazing richness in the gravy.

IRISH STEW
WITH BEEF & GUINNESS

SERVES 4

400ml Guinness
500g diced beef
1 onion, chopped
4 carrots, chopped
  (skin left on)
handful of fresh thyme
1 tbsp tomato purée
2–3 beef stock cubes
600ml boiling water
  (or less if you prefer)
1 tsp curry powder

1–2 bay leaves
3 garlic cloves, chopped
7 potatoes, peeled and
  quartered
gravy granules or 1 heaped
  tbsp of cornflour, mixed to
  a paste with 1 tbsp water
  (optional)
fresh parsley, to garnish
  (optional)
salt and pepper, to taste

1 Place all the ingredients in the slow cooker, stir and season to taste. Cook on high for 4 hours or low for 8–9 hours, then use a spoon to break up some of the potatoes into the sauce. Garnish with chopped fresh parsley, if using.

All you need is crusty bread with butter, and lots of it.

If you like a thick sauce, add the gravy granules or cornflour paste, but I prefer mine without.

Orzo has a beautiful texture and is easy to use in a whole range of different recipes. Here it is teamed with spicy roasted squash in a simple but filling dish which is truly delicious and another of my favourites. I have a veggie day every week and this is often on the menu. Other types of squash could also be used.

HARISSA-ROASTED SQUASH
WITH ORZO

SERVES 4

1 butternut squash, halved and deseeded
2 tbsp harissa paste
1 tsp paprika
1 tbsp honey
handful of fresh coriander
4 garlic cloves, crushed
1 onion, chopped

350g dried orzo pasta
850ml vegetable stock
1 tsp curry powder
500g passata
2 tbsp low-fat soft cream cheese
2 handfuls of spinach
salt and pepper, to taste

1 Chop the squash into chunky wedges and place on a baking sheet with the harissa, paprika and honey. Season to taste and toss to coat evenly. Cook in a preheated oven at 180°C for 25 minutes.

2 Peel the skin off the squash, chop the flesh and place in the slow cooker with all the remaining ingredients, except the soft cheese and spinach, and cook on high for 50 minutes. Stir and check if the pasta is cooked – if not, cook for another 15 minutes. Stir in the soft cheese and spinach.

COMFORT FOOD

You will notice that curries crop up regularly throughout this book and I won't be stopping anytime soon. Beef in a curry is simply gorgeous and the red chilli and peanut butter really elevate the sauce to an entirely new level. This classic curry will fill you up and warm you on a cold night. Add two tins of tomatoes if you like lots of sauce.

BEEF CURRY

SERVES 4

500g diced beef
150ml beef stock
1 red chilli, sliced
1 tbsp smooth peanut butter
1 onion, sliced
2 tbsp curry powder
1 tbsp garam masala
1 tbsp ground cumin
4 garlic cloves, crushed

400g tin of chopped
  tomatoes
2 tbsp tomato purée
handful of fresh coriander,
  chopped
salt and pepper, to taste
sliced chilli, fresh coriander
  and chopped peanuts,
  to garnish

1 Place all the ingredients in the slow cooker, stir and season to taste. Cook on high for 4 hours or low for 7 hours. Garnish with sliced chilli, coriander and chopped nuts.

Serve with rice and naan.

Now this is a hug in a bowl, the perfect filling dish to feed a family on one of those cold winter nights. Nothing compares to dipping butter-slathered bread into a casserole like this when the weather is miserable. I've used cocktail sausages here but you could use large sausages if you prefer. Add the cornflour paste if you like a thicker sauce. *(Recipe photo on next page.)*

SAUSAGE & BABY POTATO CASSEROLE

SERVES 4

500g cocktail sausages
1kg baby potatoes, halved
    (skin left on)
1 onion, chopped
400g tin of chopped
    tomatoes
4 garlic cloves, chopped
handful of fresh thyme
2 tbsp tomato purée
2 tbsp Worcestershire sauce
2 tbsp paprika

a few bay leaves
450ml beef stock
150ml red wine
3 carrots, chopped
    (skin left on)
1 tsp dried oregano
1 heaped tbsp cornflour,
    mixed to a paste
    with 1 tbsp water
    (optional)
salt and pepper, to taste

1 Heat a nonstick frying pan over a medium heat on the hob, then place the sausages in the pan and cook for 5–10 minutes until browned all over but not cooked through. Place the sausages and all the remaining ingredients in the slow cooker, stir and season to taste. Cook on high for 4 hours or low for 8 hours.

All you need is some nice crusty bread with butter for dipping to help it all come together.

Sausage & baby
potato casserole

502 CALORIES PER SERVING

I first tried this dish in Paris and instantly fell in love with it. I'd never made it before but after watching a Julia Child documentary, I knew I needed to make my own low-calorie slowcooker version. This is a timeless classic and can be enjoyed all year round. Perfect for any night of the week.

BEEF BOURGUIGNON

SERVES 6

200g smoked bacon, chopped
1kg diced beef
250ml red wine
2 red onions or shallots, chopped
1 tbsp low-fat butter
handful of fresh thyme
handful of fresh rosemary, chopped
2 bay leaves

450g mushrooms (left whole)
1 tbsp cornflour, mixed to a paste with 1 tbsp water
1 beef stock pot
3 carrots, chopped
4 garlic cloves, crushed
1 tbsp tomato purée
salt and pepper, to taste
chopped fresh parsley, to garnish

1 If you have time, heat a nonstick frying pan over a high heat on the hob, then place the bacon and beef in the pan and sear until just browned all over. If you're in a hurry, just skip this step.

2 Place the bacon with all the remaining ingredients in the slow cooker, stir and season to taste. Cook on low for 7–8 hours. Garnish with parsley.

Serve this rich and filling dish with potatoes of your choice.

COMFORT FOOD

I know the calorie count here is a little higher but I believe balance in your diet is perfectly healthy and actually essential. This recipe is another fan favourite and I wouldn't have been able to sleep at night if I didn't include it in this book. I love chocolate truffles, and this is a fantastic festive crowd pleaser if you're hosting friends and family. I use Lindt Lindor truffles but you can use any brand you prefer.

INDULGENT HOT CHOCOLATE

SERVES 7–8

200g dark chocolate truffles
100g milk chocolate truffles
250ml double cream

1 litre milk
a little finely grated orange
zest (optional)

1 Place all the ingredients in the slow cooker, stir and cook on high for 2 hours. Stir and check all the chocolate has melted – it may take more or less time, depending on your slow cooker.

I usually serve this luxurious hot chocolate with marshmallows, squirty cream and an extra truffle on the top. Three marshmallows add 76 calories and 12g of squirty cream adds another 28 calories.

Is there anything more festive than mulled cider? I love filling the house with those wonderful aromas and the slow cooker seems to intensify the flavour and smell. Every year I make this recipe, my online followers fall in love with it all over again. You can use wine instead of cider if you prefer, just leave out the apples. This is perfect if you are hosting and want to serve your guests something spiced and warming.

MULLED CIDER

SERVES 7

6 cloves
2 apples, sliced
2 litres cider
4–5 tbsp dark brown sugar
4 strips of orange zest
3 star anise

3 cardamoms
¼ nutmeg, grated
2 cinnamon sticks
1 vanilla pod, halved
juice from 2 clementines

1 Push the cloves into the apple slices and place in the slow cooker with all the remaining ingredients. Cook on high for 2 hours. To keep warm while serving, turn onto the low or keep warm setting if your slow cooker has one.

COMFORT FOOD

You need to try this wonderful fudge, made with just three ingredients. This is comfort food at its finest, best served with a nice cup of tea on the sofa. A lot of my online followers have made this fudge with their kids to get them involved in home cooking, which is not hard when it tastes as good as this. *(Recipe photo on next page.)*

MINI EGG FUDGE

MAKES 10 BIG SQUARES

400g milk chocolate
400g tin of condensed milk

150g Mini Eggs, chopped

1 Place the chocolate and condensed milk in the slow cooker and cook on high for 1 hour. Add the chopped Mini Eggs, stir and top with a few more. Allow to cool, then chill in the fridge for 6 hours or overnight. Turn out and cut into 10 squares.

Mini egg fudge

FEEDING
A CROWD

One of my favourite Irish soups, and one with very few ingredients. This makes a great starter for a dinner party, and you can get it ready in advance before warming it through just before your guests sit down to eat. Normally you'd soften the leeks in butter or oil but this alternative version reduces the calories. The recipe is so simple that it lives in my head rent free.

POTATO & LEEK SOUP

SERVES 6

3 potatoes, chopped
(skin left on)
3 leeks, chopped
3 garlic cloves, chopped

1 onion, chopped
1.2 litres chicken stock
150ml milk
salt and pepper, to taste

1 Place all the ingredients in the slow cooker, stir and season to taste. Cook on high for 2½–3 hours, then blitz the soup with a handheld blender until smooth.

This makes a change from a normal stew and will give you a real boost during cold and wet weather. You could brown the chorizo in a frying pan before placing in the slow cooker, but it's not really necessary with this recipe. I tasted a Spanish stew for the first time in Spain (funnily enough) and always thought it would be lovely to try my own at home in the slow cooker. This is the result.

CHORIZO AND KIDNEY BEAN STEW

SERVES 4

200g chorizo, sliced
900g potatoes, peeled
  and chopped
400g tin of chopped
  tomatoes
400g tin of kidney beans,
  drained
4 garlic cloves, crushed
juice of 1 lemon

1 tsp ground cumin
1 tsp curry powder
1 tsp paprika
½ tsp celery salt
1 onion, chopped
2 chicken stock pots
450ml boiling water
salt and pepper,
  to taste

1 Place all the ingredients in the slow cooker, stir and season to taste. Cook on high for 3 hours or low for 7 hours. Use a spoon to break up some of the potatoes to help thicken the sauce, then cook on high for another hour.

I am lucky enough to have visited Mexico and the food there makes my soul sing. This stew always goes down a treat and has layers and layers of flavour. If you can't get a tin of chipotles in adobo, use chipotle paste instead and add a handful of sliced mini peppers.

MEXICAN CHICKEN STEW
WITH GUACAMOLE

SERVES 4

4 chicken breasts, cut
   into chunks
1 red pepper, chopped
1 red onion, sliced
200g tin of chipotles in
   adobo
200g tin of sliced jalapeños,
   drained
400g tin of chopped
   tomatoes
125ml chicken stock
1 tsp ground cinnamon
1 tsp ancho chilli flakes

1 tsp ground coriander
1 tbsp paprika
4 garlic cloves, chopped
1 tbsp cornflour, mixed to
   a paste with 1 tbsp water
1 tbsp tomato purée
salt and pepper, to taste
lime wedges and fresh
   coriander, to garnish
1 quantity of Guacamole
   (see recipe on page 87),
   to serve

1 Place all the ingredients for the stew in the slow cooker, stir and season to taste. Cook on high for 3 hours or low for 5 hours.

2 Garnish the stew with lime wedges and coriander, and serve with the guacamole on the side.

You could use this as a fajita filling but I love it with lime rice. If you have some tortilla chips, use them to scoop up some of that sauce and thank me later.

               FEEDING A CROWD

I first heard of this dish on a TV show where it was being cooked by a fictional character – I googled it straight away to see what it was and was instantly intrigued. I have evolved this recipe over time and this is how I make mine today. If I'm in a hurry, I make it in a saucepan with chopped tomatoes but this slow-cooker version is such a treat.

SAUSAGE SPAGHETTI PUTTANESCA

SERVES 4

A mixture of different olives makes it look and taste amazing. You could make a veggie version of this by omitting the sausages and anchovies.

8 low-fat pork sausages
1 heaped tbsp capers
8 pitted Kalamata olives, roughly chopped
small handful of whole green or black olives
1 shallot or red onion, finely chopped
5 garlic cloves, sliced
4 anchovy fillets from a tin, finely chopped

700g passata
2 tbsp tomato purée
handful of fresh basil leaves
1 tsp dried oregano
½ tsp chilli flakes
salt and pepper, to taste
extra fresh basil and grated Parmesan cheese, to garnish
600g cooked spaghetti or fettucine, to serve

1 Heat a nonstick frying pan over a medium heat on the hob, then place the sausages in the pan and cook for 5–10 minutes until browned all over but not cooked through. Slice the sausages and place them and all the remaining ingredients in the slow cooker, stir and season to taste. Cook on high for 3 hours or low for 5 hours.

2 Stir the cooked spaghetti into the sauce or serve the sauce on top of the spaghetti. Sprinkle with basil leaves and grated Parmesan.

FEEDING A CROWD

When the weather's good, it really puts me in the mood for paella. This lazy slowcooker version is perfect for busy people – you could even make it in a saucepan if you are short on time. This is not just a summer dish – I make it all year round and now you have this slowcooker recipe, I know you will be doing the same.

CHICKEN & CHORIZO RICE

SERVES 4

100g chorizo, sliced
3 chicken breasts, cut
    into chunks
1 tsp paprika
1 tsp ground turmeric
1 tsp crushed garlic
    or garlic purée
1 tsp chilli powder
juice of 1 lemon
1 onion, chopped
400g tin of chopped
    tomatoes

900ml chicken stock
handful of fresh parsley,
    chopped
350g paella rice
1 red pepper, chopped
150g frozen peas
salt and pepper, to taste
lemon slices and extra
    chopped fresh parsley,
    to garnish

1 If you have time, heat a nonstick frying pan over a high heat on the hob, then place the chorizo in the pan and sear until just browned all over. If you're in a hurry, just skip this step.

2 Place the chorizo in the slow cooker with all the remaining ingredients, except the rice, red pepper and peas, stir and season to taste. Cook on high for 2½–3 hours or low for 6 hours. Add the rice, red pepper and peas and cook for another hour. Stir and check if the rice is cooked – if not, cook for another 15 minutes. Garnish with lemon slices and parsley.

This is one of my signature meals and something I often serve to friends. You will need a 6.5-litre slowcooker to take a shoulder of lamb, but this recipe could be cooked in the oven for 3 hours instead.

GARAM MASALA-SPICED LAMB

SERVES 7

1.5kg shoulder of lamb
1 tbsp oil
1 tbsp garam masala
1 tsp ground turmeric
handful of fresh coriander
1 tbsp curry paste (rogan josh is my favourite)

300ml lamb, chicken or beef stock
3 garlic cloves, crushed
1 onion, chopped
salt and pepper, to taste

1 Score a few deep cuts into the thickest parts of the lamb then rub all over with the oil, garam masala and turmeric. Heat a nonstick frying pan over a high heat on the hob, then place the lamb in the pan and sear on all sides until just browned all over.

2 Place all the remaining ingredients in the slow cooker, stir, then turn the meat in the liquid to coat and season to taste. Cook on low for 5 hours if you like pink lamb, or 6–7 hours if you like it well cooked.

I serve this with flatbreads, salad, yogurt and pomegranate and it is exceptional.

A cassoulet is a slow-cooked mixture of duck, pork and beans originating in the South of France and I once went to a French cookery class where I was taught how to make it. The flavour is incredible and cooking it low and slow makes it sing even louder. Some versions have breadcrumbs on top but I think crumbling some stuffing over the top takes it to another level.

DUCK CASSOULET

SERVES 4

4 duck legs
130g diced pancetta
600ml chicken stock
300ml white wine
1 celery stick, chopped
2 carrots, chopped
   (skin left on)
400g tin of butter beans,
   drained
5 garlic cloves, sliced

4 sprigs of fresh rosemary
4 sprigs of fresh thyme
2 bay leaves
1 large onion, sliced
400g tin of chopped
   tomatoes
large handful of prepared
   stuffing or breadcrumbs
   (optional)
salt and pepper, to taste

1 If you have time, heat a nonstick frying pan over a high heat on the hob, then place the duck in the pan and sear for 1–2 minutes until just browned all over. Transfer the duck to the slow cooker and repeat with the pancetta. If you're in a hurry, just skip this step.

2 Place the pancetta and all the remaining ingredients, except the stuffing or breadcrumbs, in the slow cooker, stir and season to taste. Cook on low for 6–7 hours, adding an extra hour if you didn't brown the meat.

3 If you like a crispy topping and you have an ovenproof slow cooker pot, sprinkle the stuffing or breadcrumbs over the top of the cassoulet and cook under a preheated grill until golden.

I first tried this combination of flavours in a burger and decided to recreate it with pork. Slow-cooked pork is so versatile and can be used as a base for many different meals. I am sure this will become a household favourite.

SWEET AND SPICY PORK

SERVES 4

700g boneless pork shoulder, thinly sliced
1 onion, thinly sliced
3 tbsp gochujang chilli paste
1 tbsp sesame oil
4 tbsp ketchup
6 tbsp soy sauce
100ml chicken stock
1 tbsp hoisin sauce

2 tbsp honey
5 garlic cloves, crushed
1 tsp ground ginger
2 tbsp Chinese rice wine
1 tbsp cornflour, mixed to a paste with 1 tbsp water
sliced spring onions, to garnish

1 Place all the ingredients in the slow cooker and stir. Cook on high for 3 hours or low for 4–5 hours. Garnish with spring onions.

I usually serve this pork with rice, but it's also great with tacos or wraps. Including 200g rice per serving adds 260 calories.

PER SERVING
333
CALORIES

I was first introduced to this recipe by a friend and it's addictive – once you make it you will want it time and time again. I love layering it up with soft tacos – oh my – and on occasion, I must confess I have made the largest burritos known to man. The flavour of this beef in a burrito is next level.

BARBACOA BEEF

SERVES 8

1 tbsp oil
1.5kg beef brisket, cut into large chunks (most cuts of beef will work as it falls apart)
150ml apple cider vinegar
300ml beef stock
4 garlic cloves, sliced
4 chipotles in adobo from a tin or 1 tbsp chipotle paste

1 red chilli, finely chopped
2 cloves, crushed
2 bay leaves
1 tbsp brown sugar
1 tbsp tomato purée
juice of 3 limes
1 tbsp ground cumin
1 tsp dried basil
1 tsp dried oregano
salt and pepper, to taste

1 Heat the oil in a nonstick frying pan over a high heat on the hob, then place the beef in the pan and sear for about a minute until just browned all over. Place the beef and all the remaining ingredients in the slow cooker, stir and season to taste. Cook on high for 4 hours or low for 8 hours, which results in a better flavour.

This beef is quite versatile and can be served with rice, nachos, soft tacos, chips or even a salad.

This is a divine, calorie-friendly stew with a sweet twist – the addition of prunes. Not a common ingredient in a stew, the prunes give a real depth and sweetness to the sauce and help thicken it too, but you can easily leave them out if you're not a fan. Another fantastic winter warmer for a midweek meal with friends.

BEEF, SWEET POTATO & SPINACH STEW

SERVES 4

1kg sweet potatoes, chopped
600g diced beef
6 pitted prunes, chopped (optional)
1 onion, chopped
4 garlic cloves, crushed
2 bay leaves
1 tbsp paprika
400g tin of chopped tomatoes

2 tbsp tomato purée
500ml beef stock
handful of fresh parsley, chopped
handful of fresh thyme
1 tbsp cornflour, mixed to a paste with 1 tbsp water
large handful of spinach
salt and pepper, to taste

1 Place all the ingredients, except the spinach, in the slow cooker, stir and season to taste. Cook on high for 4–5 hours, then stir in the spinach.

Serve with some nice crusty bread for mopping up the sweet sauce.

When I asked my friends if they cook lamb at home, 90 per cent of them said no, yet there are so many brilliant recipes you can rustle up, it is probably the most flavoursome meat. It is especially good paired with spices in this delicious dish, which gets its inspiration from a traditional Moroccan tagine. Like the cone-shaped tagine, the slow cooker retains moisture while the lamb cooks and makes the meat so tender.

SPICED APRICOT LAMB

SERVES 4

600g lean diced lamb
1 tbsp oil
1–2 tbsp mild curry powder
1 tbsp ground turmeric
1 onion, sliced
2 carrots, finely chopped
2 x 400g tins of chopped
    tomatoes
50g dried apricots, finely
    chopped
1 tbsp tomato purée
1 tsp ground cinnamon or
    1 cinnamon stick

5 garlic cloves, crushed
5cm fresh ginger, grated
500ml chicken stock
1 tbsp honey
handful of fresh coriander,
    chopped
3 fresh mint leaves, chopped
    (optional)
salt and pepper, to taste
chopped fresh coriander,
    mint leaves and flaked
    almonds, to garnish

Serve with a spoonful of yogurt, some salad and couscous or potato wedges.

1 If you have time, rub the lamb all over with the oil, curry powder and turmeric. Heat a nonstick frying pan over a high heat on the hob, then place the lamb and onion in the pan and sear on all sides for 1–2 minutes until just browned all over. If you're in a hurry, just skip this step.

2 Place the lamb with all the remaining ingredients in the slow cooker, stir and season to taste. Cook on low for 4–5 hours. Garnish with coriander, mint and flaked almonds.

I created this recipe last year as I cook brisket all the time in the slow cooker but I thought I'd try it with mulled wine for a festive vibe. The result was just delicious, with a mild sweetness and super-rich depth of flavour. I find the slow cooker elevates any flavour to an entirely new level.

MULLED WINE BRISKET

SERVES 6

1kg piece of beef brisket
1 carrot, chopped (skin left on)
2 bay leaves
2 sprigs of fresh rosemary
1 red onion, chopped
400g tin of chopped tomatoes

1 tbsp tomato purée
4 garlic cloves, crushed
1 cinnamon stick
400ml mulled wine
300ml rich beef stock
1 slice of orange
salt and pepper, to taste

1 Heat a nonstick frying pan over a high heat on the hob, then place the beef in the pan and sear on all sides until just browned all over. Place all the remaining ingredients in the slow cooker, stir, then turn the meat in the liquid to coat and season to taste. Cook on high for 7–8 hours. Shred the meat with two forks.

Serve with mashed potatoes and seasonal veg.

A ham is not just for Christmas – I make this all year round and the slow-cooker method takes the stress out of it. Soak the ham overnight in cold water to take the salt out before cooking. I'll let you into a little secret – I always buy an extra-large ham so there are plenty of succulent leftovers to keep me in sandwiches for days afterwards.

HONEY & MUSTARD HAM
IN CIDER

SERVES 10

2 large oranges, sliced
1.5kg boneless gammon joint
20–25 cloves
1 cinnamon stick
1 star anise

1 bay leaf
500ml cider
6 tbsp honey
1 tbsp mustard

1 Place half the orange slices in the bottom of the slow cooker and place the ham on top. Add the cloves, cinnamon, star anise, bay leaf and cider and cook on high for 4–5 hours or low for 7–8 hours. Allow to cool. You can also stud the ham with cloves for extra flavour, if you like.

2 Place the remaining orange slices in an ovenproof dish and place the ham on top. Trim the skin and/or fat off the ham until just a thin layer of fat remains, then score it in a criss-cross pattern. Brush the ham with the honey and mustard, then cook in an oven preheated to 190˚C for 25–30 minutes, basting every 10 minutes.

A ham this size is a tight squeeze in a 3.5-litre slow cooker, so you might need a larger slow cooker for this dish.

Who doesn't love a good Sunday roast? When I was growing up, my Mum always made her Sunday roast in the slow cooker, so this dish is inspired by her. It takes the stress out of cooking for a large group, but there is no compromise on flavour. A piece of beef this size is a tight squeeze in my 3.5-litre slow cooker, so you might need a larger model if you are feeding a crowd.

SUNDAY ROAST & GRAVY

SERVES 10–11

1.5kg beef roasting joint
1 onion, chopped
1 carrot, chopped
  (skin left on)
handful of fresh rosemary
100ml rich beef stock

2 garlic cloves, peeled
gravy granules or 1 heaped
  tbsp of cornflour, mixed to
  a paste with 1 tbsp water
  (optional)
salt and pepper, to taste

1 Heat a nonstick frying pan over a high heat on the hob, then place the beef in the pan and sear on all sides until just browned all over. Place all the remaining ingredients, except the gravy granules or cornflour paste, in the slow cooker, stir, then turn the meat in the liquid to coat and season to taste. Cook on low for 6 hours.

2 I like my beef to be pink in the middle, but everyone likes theirs done differently. Slice into the beef to check if you are happy – if not, cook for longer then check again.

3 Remove the beef from the slow cooker and use the cooking juices to make gravy. Either stir the cornflour paste into the juices to thicken or add the gravy granules for an ultra-rich gravy. Serve with potatoes, carrots and lots of green veg.

INDEX

ACKNOWLEDGEMENTS

I would like to dedicate this book to my online followers. Without the continued support of whom, I don't think I'd be writing this book today. Thank you to each and every one of you.

DON'T MISS MY NEXT BOOK

PUBLISHING IN SPRING 2023

1 3 5 7 9 10 8 6 4 2

Published in 2023 by Ebury Press
an imprint of Ebury Publishing,
20 Vauxhall Bridge Road,
London SW1V 2SA

Ebury Press is part of the Penguin Random House group
of companies whose addresses can be found at global.
penguinrandomhouse.com

First published by Ebury Press in 2023

www.penguin.co.uk

A CIP catalogue record for this book is available from the British
Library

ISBN 9781529903546

Photography: Clare Wilkinson
Food and prop styling: Charlotte O'Connell
Styling assistant: Susan Willis
Design: maru studio

Printed and bound in Italy by Graphicom S.p.A.
The authorised representative in the EEA is Penguin Random House
Ireland, Morrison Chambers, 32 Nassau Street, Dublin D02 YH68.